POCKET
MANUAL

The world's most dangerous animals

DEADLY CREATURES

Haynes
®

DEADLY CREATURES
CONTENTS

LOXODONTA AFRICANA
AFRICAN ELEPHANT

The African elephant is the largest and heaviest land animal in the world. Its huge ears, long trunk and curved tusks add to its impressive appearance. Due to the destruction of their habitat they often wander onto farmland where they come into conflict with people. This makes them one of the most dangerous animals to humans in Africa.

VITAL STATISTICS

BODY HEIGHT:	2.4–3.3m
WEIGHT:	3000–6000kg
EATS:	leaves, grasses, bark
LIFESPAN:	50–60 years
HABITAT:	grasslands, forests
DISTRIBUTION:	

WARNING

Elephants do not attack other animals for food. But they can be very aggressive when they are protecting calves or when males fight each other. An elephant warns another animal by trumpeting and spreading its ears. If this does not work, it charges at anything in its path. The elephant can terrify any animal it sees as a threat by growling, roaring and screaming.

DID YOU KNOW?

An elephant's trunk has around 100,000 muscles in it. The elephant uses it to drink, breathe, smell, trumpet and pick things up.

DEADLY FEATURES

An elephant's huge size makes it a formidable opponent. Its intelligence and speed make it extra deadly. It can trample and crush any other animal that it sees as a threat. It also uses its tusks as weapons in a fight.

DEADLY RATING

SYNCERUS CAFFER CAFFER
AFRICAN CAPE BUFFALO

Herds of African buffalo wander the savanna, grazing on the grass. These huge beasts are closely related to cows but are considered to be one of the most dangerous animals in Africa. To defend themselves, and their calves, buffaloes will stand up to fierce predators, including lions.

VITAL STATISTICS

BODY LENGTH:	up to 3m
WEIGHT:	300–900kg
EATS:	grasses
LIFESPAN:	around 20 years
HABITAT:	grasslands
DISTRIBUTION:	

HORNED HERD

The buffalo is a large animal with a reputation for being bad-tempered. Sticking together in a herd gives the buffaloes safety in numbers and makes them formidable enemies. Both male and female buffaloes have huge, sharp horns, joined together by a hard plate. The male with the thickest horns leads the herd. Males use their horns to fight each other for mates and to decide who is in charge.

DID YOU KNOW?

The buffalo is known as one of the 'Big Five' animals on the African savanna. The other four are the lion, leopard, rhinoceros and elephant.

DEADLY FEATURES

The buffalo's huge size, power and speed help it to scare away enemies. Although normally quiet and calm, if it has to fight, the herd can charge at high speed, trampling other animals under hooves and goring them with horns.

DEADLY RATING

PYTHON SEBAE
AFRICAN ROCK PYTHON

Africa's largest snake, the African rock python has a massive muscular body and lives in a wide range of habitats. Because of its size, it spends most of its time on the ground, but it is also an excellent swimmer and will often ambush prey from the water's edge.

⚠ VITAL STATISTICS

BODY LENGTH:	5–6m
WEIGHT:	up to 90kg
EATS:	monkeys, antelope, lizards, crocodiles
LIFESPAN:	25 years
HABITAT:	savannas, rivers, forests
DISTRIBUTION:	

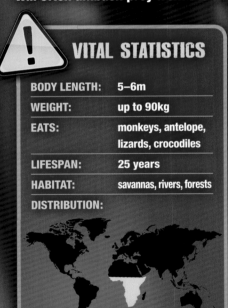

KILLER COILS

African rock pythons kill their prey by constriction. They normally hunt wild animals, although if they live close to humans they have been known to kill goats, chickens, dogs and other domestic pets. A rock python hunts its prey at dusk, using its heat-sensing organs. It sits and waits, until an animal comes close. Then it strikes, gripping its victim in its teeth and coiling its body around it. Every time its victim breathes out, the snake tightens its grip.

DEADLY RATING

DEADLY FEATURES

DID YOU KNOW?

Female African rock pythons are caring parents. The female lays her eggs in an empty burrow or termite mound. Then she coils around the eggs to protect them.

With its huge body and powerful coils, this snake can constrict an animal as large as a 60kg antelope. It also has large, curved teeth and can give a very painful bite. It is known to be bad-tempered and will readily bite, if provoked.

ALLIGATOR MISSISSIPPIENSIS
AMERICAN ALLIGATOR

Alligators can be told apart from crocodiles by their rounded snouts and the fact that their lower teeth do not stick out when their mouths are closed. The American alligator lives in freshwater swamps, rivers and lakes in the USA. It has a powerful, armour-plated body, with a long tail and webbed feet.

VITAL STATISTICS

BODY LENGTH:	3–4.5m
WEIGHT:	up to 500kg
EATS:	fish, mammals
LIFESPAN:	35–50 years
HABITAT:	swamps, rivers, lakes

DISTRIBUTION:

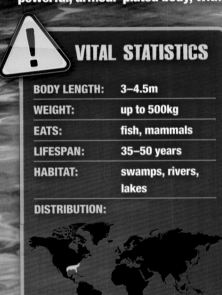

RIVER HUNTER

Lying in the water, the alligator looks like a floating log...until its prey comes close. Young alligators start off by eating shrimps, snails and insects, but adults hunt fish, frogs, snakes and mammals. American alligators hunt mainly at night, snapping up prey in the water. They also catch animals that come to drink at the water's edge.

DID YOU KNOW?

In the dry season, alligators dig holes in the ground, using their snouts and tails. These 'alligator holes' fill with water and make a welcome hiding place from the heat.

DEADLY FEATURES

An American alligator's huge jaws are lined with up to 80 sharp, conical teeth and it has the strongest bite possibly of any animal. It grabs its prey in a vice-like grip, then holds on to it until it drowns.

DEADLY RATING

☠☠

PANTHERA TIGRIS TIGRIS
BENGAL TIGER

The tiger is the largest and strongest of all the big cats. This magnificent predator hunts at night, using the camouflage of its striped coat to hide among the shadows. Sadly, the tiger is now endangered because people have hunted it for its skin and body parts, and destroyed its habitat.

VITAL STATISTICS

BODY LENGTH:	2.4–3.1m
WEIGHT:	100–260kg
EATS:	buffalo, deer, antelope, wild pigs
LIFESPAN:	up to 15 years
HABITAT:	forests, woodland
DISTRIBUTION:	

INCREDIBLE CAT

The Bengal tiger lives in the forests of India, Bangladesh, Nepal and China. It lives alone except for when a female has cubs. The tiger marks its large territory with scent to keep other tigers away. It has very strong senses of sight, smell and hearing that help it to find prey. Tigers can jump over 9 metres, are good at climbing trees and, unlike other big cats, are excellent swimmers.

ENDANGERED · SPECIES

TIGER DANGER

DID YOU KNOW?

A tiger's roar is very loud. It can be heard as far as 3 kilometres away! This warns other tigers away from one tiger's territory. Like a pet cat, a tiger will purr when it is happy.

Over the last 100 years, tiger numbers have fallen from hundreds of thousands to fewer than 3,000. This is because the tigers' habitat has been destroyed and they have been hunted for their body parts which are used in traditional Chinese medicine.

TERRIFYING HUNTER

The tiger's strength and speed alone make it a fearsome hunter. Its thick neck and powerful front paws make it strong enough to hold down and drag heavy prey. Its orange and black stripes blend in with shadows of the forest, so its victims cannot see it until it is too late. The tiger lies very still until a victim comes near. Then it creeps slowly forwards until it is close enough to jump on its prey and grip it in its jaws.

DID YOU KNOW?

Female tigers have two to six cubs in each litter. The cubs stay with their mother, learning to hunt, for up to three years.

DEADLY FEATURES

The tiger's camouflage means it can take its prey by surprise. It has strong, sharp teeth and claws for pulling its victims to the ground. If the animal is small, the tiger breaks its neck in its powerful jaws. It kills a larger animal by biting its throat.

DEADLY RATING

URSUS AMERICANUS
BLACK BEAR

The American black bear is the most common type of bear. A different type of black bear can be found in Asia. They mostly eat berries and grasses, but they also feed on insects and some animals. They are excellent tree climbers.

VITAL STATISTICS

BODY LENGTH:	up to 2m
WEIGHT:	40–400kg
EATS:	roots, fruit, insects, fish, deer, birds
LIFESPAN:	10–25 years
HABITAT:	forests, meadows
DISTRIBUTION:	

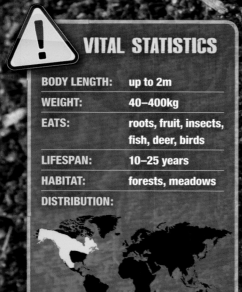

DANGER

Black bears live alone except for when females are looking after cubs. If a mother bear feels threatened, she sends her cubs to safety up a tree before attacking. Some black bears hunt and kill deer or moose calves. Others catch fish at night when they cannot be easily seen by their prey. Generally, black bears will only attack people if they are threatened.

DID YOU KNOW?

Not all black bears are black! Some have light brown, grey or even white coats. This may be because they need to be differently camouflaged in different habitats.

DEADLY FEATURES

The black bear is very powerful and will protect its food or young against any threat. A strong swipe with a paw can do serious damage. Generally, though, the bears are more frightened of people than the other way round.

DEADLY RATING

DENDROASPIS POLYLEPIS
BLACK MAMBA

One of the world's most venomous snakes, the black mamba lives in southern and eastern Africa. It is found in rocky hills or wooded savanna where it hides inside termite mounds and hollow trees or basks in the sun. It gets its name from the black colouring inside its mouth, though its skin is actually olive green or brownish-grey.

VITAL STATISTICS

BODY LENGTH:	2.5–4m
WEIGHT:	1.5kg
EATS:	rodents, small birds
LIFESPAN:	12 years
HABITAT:	forests, grasslands
DISTRIBUTION:	

DEADLY STRIKE

From the same family as cobras, the black mamba is five times as venomous as a king cobra. It uses its poison to kill its prey of rodents and small birds. Usually shy and secretive, it can be particularly dangerous if it is cornered or threatened. Then it raises its head off the ground, opens its mouth wide and flicks out its tongue, then hisses before striking.

DEADLY RATING

DID YOU KNOW?

The black mamba is the fastest-moving snake on land. At top speed, it can move at 20 kilometres per hour for short bursts, especially if it is trying to avoid danger. It can also climb trees.

DEADLY FEATURES

A black mamba's venom is deadly. It strikes its prey several times at speed, then waits for it to become paralysed and die, before swallowing it whole. Its bite could kill a human being in 20 minutes, unless treated with anti-venom.

LATRODECTUS SP.
BLACK WIDOW SPIDER

There are around 30 species of black widow spider that live in many warm places around the world, and they have a fearsome reputation. Female black widows are some of the most venomous spiders in the world. These spiders are especially common in North America and sometimes live close to towns and cities.

VITAL STATISTICS

BODY LENGTH:	up to 10mm
WEIGHT:	approx 1g
EATS:	insects, other spiders
LIFESPAN:	females: up to 3 years
	males: up to 2 months
HABITAT:	woodlands, urban areas
DISTRIBUTION:	

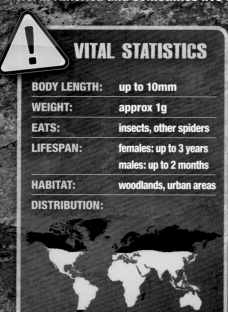

LYING IN WAIT

The black widow spider lives alone and makes its web close to the ground or under ledges, plants or rocks. It often puts this tunnel-like web in dark spaces and spends the daytime hiding inside, lying in wait. The spider's prey crawls into the inviting dark hole and then the black widow strikes. When it sees prey on its web, the spider uses special bristles on its legs to cover its victim in sticky silk.

DID YOU KNOW?

Female black widows are famous for eating male spiders after they have mated. In reality, this does not happen very often. Male black widows are much smaller and often have markings on their backs.

SPIDER EGGS

After mating, a female spider lays up to 750 eggs, in little bunches. Each bunch is laid inside a paper-like eggs sac and hung on the web to protect it from predators.

DINNER TIME

Once its prey is trapped in the web, the black widow spider bites its victim and injects it with venom. The spider then drags its dead victim into a safe part of the web to eat. The black widow chews its prey and fills it with special juices from its fangs. These juices, called enzymes, turn its prey's body to mush which the spider then sucks up. The black widow mainly eats insects and other bugs, but will also sometimes eat small mice and lizards.

DID YOU KNOW?
Many female black widow spiders have a shiny black body with a red marking shaped like an hourglass on their underside. This bright marking warns predators that the spider is venomous.

DEADLY FEATURES

The black widow spider has venom around 15 times more powerful than a rattlesnake. Although a black widow bite is not normally fatal for humans, it can kill many animals.

HAPALOCHLAENA SP.
BLUE-RINGED OCTOPUS

Compared to many other octopuses, the blue-ringed octopus is tiny. Measuring up to 20 centimetres across, it can easily sit on your hand. Yet it is one of the deadliest creatures in the sea, capable of killing a human with its venomous bite.

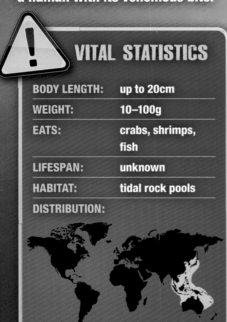

VITAL STATISTICS

BODY LENGTH:	up to 20cm
WEIGHT:	10–100g
EATS:	crabs, shrimps, fish
LIFESPAN:	unknown
HABITAT:	tidal rock pools
DISTRIBUTION:	

OCTOPUS LIFESTYLE

The blue-ringed octopus lives in rock pools along the coast around Australia and in the western Pacific region. It is easy to recognise by the blue and black rings on its yellow body. The octopus is shy, hiding away in cracks and holes. It will only attack humans if it is stepped on or picked up. Its usual prey is small crabs, shrimps and sometimes fish.

The blue-ringed octopus can change colour to blend in with its surroundings. Its brightly coloured rings show up only when it is alarmed or provoked.

DEADLY FEATURES

A blue-ringed octopus's poison paralyses its victim so it cannot breathe. The venom can kill a human in 10–20 minutes. There is no anti-venom available. At the first sign of having been bitten, get to hospital fast.

DEADLY RATING

CHIRONEX FLECKERI
BOX JELLYFISH

As its name suggests, the box jellyfish has a box-shaped body, or bell, about the size of a football. It is not only the most venomous jellyfish but possibly the deadliest creature in the world. Four groups of tentacles trail from each corner of the bell, each covered in deadly stinging cells.

VITAL STATISTICS

BODY LENGTH:	20cm
WEIGHT:	up to 3kg
EATS:	small fish, prawns
LIFESPAN:	less than a year
HABITAT:	coasts
DISTRIBUTION:	

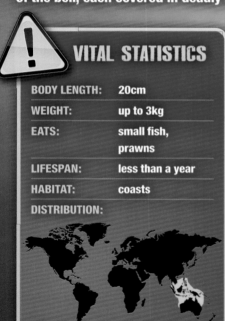

BOX BEACHES

Box jellyfish live in shallow water off the coasts of northern Australia and South East Asia. They are most commonly seen between October and April when they drift close to the shore to breed. Beaches in affected areas put up signposts warning swimmers to be careful. Nets are also put in the water, keeping the jellyfish out and the swimmers safe.

STINGER FIRST AID

DID YOU KNOW?

Box jellyfish are preyed on by sea turtles. For some reason, the turtles are able to eat box jellyfish without being stung.

If a person is stung, the wound should be washed with vinegar. This stops the stinging cells from working. Any tentacles should be carefully picked off the skin. Then the victim needs emergency medical help.

The box jellyfish is also known as the SEA WASP or MARINE STINGER

DEADLY STING

Each of the jellyfish's tentacles measures about three metres long and is covered in thousands of lethal stinging cells. These shoot tiny darts of venom into any creature that brushes past them. The jellyfish normally uses its venom to catch and kill prey but it will also sting in self defence. Box jellyfish hunt alone, during the day. At night, they rest on the sea bed.

DID YOU KNOW?

Box jellyfish are strong swimmers. They can shoot along in bursts of up to 1.8 metres per second (about 6.5 km/h) when they are hunting prey.

DEADLY FEATURES

A single box jellyfish has enough venom to kill 60 adult humans. Its sting causes excruciating pain, and death can follow in four minutes, as the fast-acting venom attacks the victim's heart and nervous system.

DEADLY RATING

PHONEUTRIA NIGRIVENTER
BRAZILIAN WANDERING SPIDER

The Brazilian wandering spider is one of the most venomous spiders in the world. Highly aggressive, it lives in Central and South America where it wanders the rainforest floor. Often wandering near to human dwellings, they may be found hiding in houses, cars and log piles.

VITAL STATISTICS

BODY LENGTH:	up to 4.8cm
WEIGHT:	unknown
EATS:	insects, mice, lizards
LIFESPAN:	up to 2 years
HABITAT:	tropical rainforest floors

DISTRIBUTION:

SPIDER PREY

The wandering spider is a large, brown, hairy spider with a leg span of up to 12.5 centimetres. It stalks and hunts its prey across the forest floor, sinking its fearsome fangs into its victims for a quick kill. When it feels threatened, the spider lifts up its front legs and shows its fangs.

DEADLY RATING

DID YOU KNOW?

The Brazilian wandering spider is sometimes called the banana spider because it has been found hiding in crates of bananas that have travelled across the world.

DEADLY FEATURES

The Brazilian wandering spider is a terrifying predator because of its aggressive nature. It often hides in dark places where humans can disturb it, and if disturbed, it will defend itself so bites to humans can be fairly frequent.

MYRMECIA
BULLDOG ANT

There are many different species of bulldog ant, and they are also known as bull ants or jumper ants. These large ants can grow to be more than 40 millimetres long, and are famous for their aggressive behaviour and painful stings. All species of bulldog ant live in Australia only.

VITAL STATISTICS

BODY LENGTH:	15–40mm
WEIGHT:	unknown
EATS:	small insects
LIFESPAN:	up to 10 weeks
HABITAT:	forests, heathland, urban areas

DISTRIBUTION:

ANT AGGRESSION

The bulldog ant can be red, orange or black. It is so strong that it can carry prey that is seven times heavier than it is. The ant uses its powerful eyesight to track down prey. It seizes a victim in its jaws and injects venom from its sting to kill it. The ants guard their nests fiercely and will attack anything that comes too close.

DEADLY RATING

💀💀💀💀

DID YOU KNOW?

Some bulldog ants are called jumper ants because they jump at anything that threatens them. They have especially strong back legs that allow them to do this.

DEADLY FEATURES

The bulldog ant's main weapons are its crushing jaws and venomous sting. Its sting can be very painful to humans but is usually only deadly if the victim is allergic to stings.

CARCHARHINUS LEUCAS
BULL SHARK

With its stocky, barrel-shaped body and fierce reputation, the bull shark lives up to its name. It is wider than most sharks its size, with plain grey markings, a blunt, rounded snout and a long, tapering back fin that makes it easy to spot. Bull sharks usually live in shallow, coastal waters in warm seas around the world.

VITAL STATISTICS

BODY LENGTH:	up to 3.5m
WEIGHT:	90–250kg
EATS:	fish, sharks, sea turtles, dolphins
LIFESPAN:	16–27 years
HABITAT:	tropical coasts
DISTRIBUTION:	

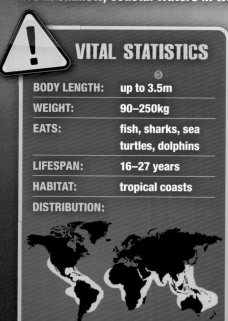

FRESHWATER SHARK

Bull sharks live along the coasts of warm and tropical oceans. Unusually for sharks, they are also able to survive in freshwater rivers and lakes as well as the salt water of the sea. Incredibly, bulls sharks have been found more than 4,000 kilometres up the River Amazon in South America. Most sharks become ill and may die in freshwater. But bull sharks are able to adapt their body chemistry by drinking lots of water.

Bull sharks found living in Lake Nicaragua in Central America reach the lake by jumping along river rapids, almost like salmon. It takes them about a week to make the journey from the sea.

SHARK DANGER

Few animals scare a bull shark, although some are preyed on by crocodiles and larger sharks. Their biggest threat comes from humans who catch them for their meat and skins.

BUMP AND BITE

A bull shark hunts alone. It swims slowly through the shallow water, then suddenly puts on a burst of speed as soon as it spots prey. It eats a wide range of sea animals, including fish, other sharks, sae turtles, sea birds and dolphins. They have also been known on rare occasions to attack land animals such as horses and even hippopotamuses. The shark uses the bump-and-bite method technique to attack prey. It circles round its victim, then head butts it before biting. It guards its territory fiercely and will also launch a vicious attack on any intruders.

💀✖💀✖💀✖💀✖💀

DEADLY FEATURES

DID YOU KNOW?

Bull sharks living in fresh water have to drink so much water to survive that they produce 20 times more urine than sharks living in salt water.

A bull shark's triangular, saw-edged teeth are lethal weapons on their own. Combined with the shark's aggressive nature, they are deadly. Bull sharks are dangerous to humans, and have been known to attack.

PUMA CONCOLOR
COUGAR

Cougars live in both North and South America and are extremely adaptable, living in a wide variety of habitats. Also known as pumas or mountain lions, these long, slim cats have sandy brown fur. Their hunting territories can cover hundreds of square kilometres.

⚠ VITAL STATISTICS

BODY LENGTH:	up to 1.5m
WEIGHT:	up to 120kg
EATS:	deer, moose, birds, mice, porcupines
LIFESPAN:	up to 13 years
HABITAT:	forests, grasslands
DISTRIBUTION:	

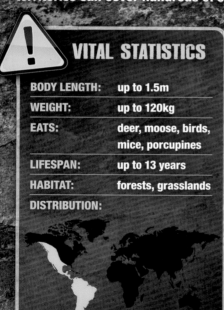

COUGAR PREY

A cougar kills prey as large as moose and caribou, or it will eat small animals such as birds, fish and squirrels. The cougar stalks its prey at night and leaps out when its victim gets close. One bite of its jaws can be enough to break an animal's neck.

DID YOU KNOW?

When a cougar makes a large kill, it drags the dead animal to a hiding place and covers it with leaves. Over the following days, it returns to its hiding place to eat more of its kill.

DEADLY FEATURES

The cougar's long, strong back legs help it to sprint and jump quickly after prey. Its powerful jaws and long, sharp teeth give its victims little chance of escape once they are in its grip.

DEADLY RATING

☠ ☠ ☠

CROTALUS ATROX
DIAMOND-BACKED RATTLESNAKE

The Western diamond-back rattlesnake lives in the south-western USA and parts of Mexico. It likes dry, rocky places where it can hide among shrubs or cracks in the rocks. It is well camouflaged by its yellowish-grey skin and is named after the dark diamond shapes running along its back.

VITAL STATISTICS

BODY LENGTH:	length: 1.5m
WEIGHT:	up to 6.7kg
EATS:	birds, small mammals, lizards
LIFESPAN:	15 years
HABITAT:	deserts, scrubland
DISTRIBUTION:	

DEADLY RATTLE

Rattlesnakes are famous for the scales at the end of their tails. They are made up of loosely attached hard plates of keratin, which is also what the hair and horns of other animals are made of. If a rattlesnake is threatened, it coils its body, ready to strike, and shakes its rattle at its attacker as a warning. The scales knock together when the tail is shaken, making an eerie, rattling sound. If its attacker is not frightened away, the snake strikes.

DID YOU KNOW?

Rattlesnakes have special heat-sensing pits on the sides of their heads that allow them to track down their prey in the dark.

DEADLY FEATURES

Rattlesnakes have long fangs and a deadly poisonous bite. They use their venom for self-defence and to catch prey. The venom kills an animal in seconds and also helps to digest its body.

DEADLY RATING

☠️ ☠️ ☠️

ELECTROPHORUS ELECTRICUS
ELECTRIC EEL

Found in the rivers of South America, the electric eel lives up to its reputation. It is the world's most powerful electric fish and a top predator. It uses electricity built up in its body to shock and kill its prey of fish and small mammals. In spite of its name, the electric eel is in fact more closely related to catfish than to ordinary freshwater eels.

VITAL STATISTICS

BODY LENGTH:	2.5m
WEIGHT:	20kg
EATS:	fish, small mammals
LIFESPAN:	unknown
HABITAT:	rivers, streams
DISTRIBUTION:	

AMAZING EELS

Electric eels have long, snake-like bodies and can grow up to 2.5 metres long. Their bodies are covered in thick, slimy skin that helps to protect the eels from their own electricity. A long fin stretches along the underside of their bodies and is used for swimming. The eels live mostly on the muddy river bottom. Unlike most fish, they do not have gills and have to rise to the surface regularly to breathe.

DEADLY RATING

☠ ☠ ☠ ☠ ☠

DID YOU KNOW?

Electric eels also use their electricity to find their way around. This is important because they not only have poor eyesight but live in dark, murky water where it is difficult to see.

DEADLY FEATURES

An electric eel has three organs in its body that make electricity. It uses an electric shock to stun its prey, then sucks it into its mouth. An eel can produce a charge of up to 500 volts and, although rare, this would be enough to kill a human.

ANDROCTONUS AUSTRALIS
FAT-TAILED SCORPION

The deadly fat-tailed scorpion lives in the deserts of the Middle East and Africa. It gets its name from its wide tail. These medium-sized scorpions can be brown, black or yellow. Like all scorpions, they have pincers at the front and a curved tail, ending in a stinger, at the back.

VITAL STATISTICS

BODY LENGTH:	10cm
WEIGHT:	unknown
EATS:	insects, spiders, lizards
LIFESPAN:	unknown
HABITAT:	deserts
DISTRIBUTION:	

DESERT HUNTER

Fat-tailed scorpions are nocturnal. During the day, they shelter from the desert heat in burrows and cracks in the rocks. At night, they come out to hunt their prey of insects, spiders and small lizards. A scorpion waits for prey to pass by, then grabs it in its pincers. Then it curls its tail over and gives its victim a poisonous sting. It also stings to defend itself against predators, such as owls, bats and large lizards.

DID YOU KNOW?
Baby scorpions climb on to their mothers' backs and ride piggy-back for about a week until they are old enough to look after themselves.

DEADLY FEATURES

A fat-tailed scorpion's poison is deadly and scorpion stings cause several human deaths each year. A scorpion can regulate how much poison it injects in a sting. If its whole supply is used up, it can take several days to make more.

DEADLY RATING

☠️✖️☠️

ATRAX ROBUSTUS
FUNNEL-WEB SPIDER

Found in Australia, the Sydney funnel-web spider is one of the deadliest spiders on Earth. There are several different types of funnel-web, the most dangerous being the Sydney funnel-web. It tends to live under rocks and fallen logs. But it also likes to wander into houses and lurk in gardens and compost heaps.

VITAL STATISTICS

BODY LENGTH:	(females) 3.5cm; (males) 2.5cm
WEIGHT:	unknown
EATS:	insects, frogs
LIFESPAN:	8 or more years
HABITAT:	forests, gardens
DISTRIBUTION:	

FUNNEL WEBS

As their name suggests, funnel-web spiders build funnel-shaped webs in the ground, under rocks or under rotting logs. In gardens, webs may be found in rockeries and sometimes lawns. A web will be approximately 30cm long and lined with silk. Silk tripwires stretch from the entrance. These warn the spiders of passing prey, mates or danger. At night, the spider sits just inside the entrance with its front legs on the trip wires.

DEADLY RATING

WANDERING MALES

DID YOU KNOW?

Funnel-webs like to burrow in damp places because their bodies can easily dry out. The only problem is that their burrows can flood if there is heavy rain.

In the summer, male funnel-webs wander about in search of a mate. They seem to be attracted to water and sometimes fall into swimming pools. They can survive for up to 24 hours by trapping air around their body.

More than 40 species of funnel-web spiders live in Australia

SPIDER APPEARANCE

Funnel-webs are medium-sized spiders, with glossy, bluish-black bodies, covered in fine, velvety hairs. Female spiders grow up to 3.5 centimetres long (not including their legs). Males are smaller and grow up to 2.5 centimetres long. Funnel-webs eat other spiders, snails and sometimes frogs which they catch at the entrance to their webs. They bite their prey to inject their poison and drag it down into the funnel to eat.

DID YOU KNOW?

A few types of funnel-web live in trees. They build their webs inside rotting tree trunks and feed on beetles and other insects.

DEADLY FEATURES

Sydney funnel-webs have large fangs that are sharp enough to bite through shoes or even human fingernails. They can be extremely aggressive and will readily bite if threatened. It is the male spider that has particularly toxic venom.

DEADLY RATING

BITIS GABONICA
GABOON VIPER

Found in the rainforests of Africa, gaboon vipers are the largest and heaviest vipers, growing up to 2 metres long. Their skin is brownish-grey with striking patterns of yellow and black diamonds, triangles and spots. These markings help to hide them as they lie among the leaves on the forest floor.

⚠ VITAL STATISTICS

BODY LENGTH:	up to 2m
WEIGHT:	up to 10kg
EATS:	rodents, birds, frogs, toads
LIFESPAN:	18 years
HABITAT:	rainforests, grasslands
DISTRIBUTION:	

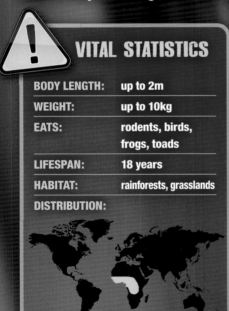

NIGHT HUNTERS

Gaboon vipers hunt alone and at night. They are most active at sunset when they start to search for their prey of rodents, birds, frogs and toads. They usually lie among the leaves, waiting for prey to pass by. Then they attack with a deadly, venomous bite.

DEADLY FEATURES

DID YOU KNOW?

Gaboon vipers can be deadly but they are usually very placid. If they are threatened, they hiss loudly but do not strike unless they are seriously provoked.

The gaboon viper has the longest fangs of any venomous snake. Its fangs measure about 5cm in length and inject large amounts of venom if they bite. To keep the fangs out of the way, they rotate back into the mouth when the mouth is closed; when the mouth opens, the fangs flick out rapidly.

CONUS GEOGRAPHUS
GEOGRAPHY CONE SHELL

The cone shell is a type of sea snail that lives on coral reefs in the Indian and Pacific Oceans. The Geography cone is creamy white with a pattern of orange or red bands or blotches. Its appearance makes it popular with shell collectors. But picking a cone shell up could be fatal – this beautiful-looking creature is deadly poisonous.

VITAL STATISTICS

BODY LENGTH:	10cm
WEIGHT:	unknown
EATS:	fish, molluscs, worms
LIFESPAN:	unknown
HABITAT:	coral reefs
DISTRIBUTION:	

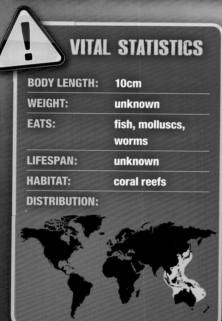

KILLER CONE

Cone shells prey on other sea animals, such as fish and worms. It detects its prey in the water with a tube-like siphon. Then it kills its victim with its lethal venom. The venom acts quickly and paralyses the prey first. This is important because the cone shell is very slow-moving and fast-swimming fish could easily get away. Once dead, the prey is sucked into the cone shell's stomach where it is digested.

DID YOU KNOW?

Scientists have discovered that some chemicals in a cone shell's venom could be used as painkillers. They are thousands of times more powerful than the strongest painkillers used today.

DEADLY FEATURES

A cone shell shoots its deadly venom into its victim through a harpoon-like tooth. There are many different types of cone shell, but some, like the Geography cone, have venom strong enough to kill a human. There is no known anti-venom.

DEADLY RATING

CARCHARODON CARCHARIAS
GREAT WHITE SHARK

Made famous in the 1970s film 'Jaws', the great white shark is one of the fiercest and most famous hunters in the sea. Its massive, streamlined body is built for speeding after prey, and it has a pointed snout, black eyes and a crescent-shaped tail.

VITAL STATISTICS

BODY LENGTH:	up to 6m
WEIGHT:	up to 3,400kg
EATS:	large fish, seals, sea lions, turtles
LIFESPAN:	approx 30 years
HABITAT:	cool, subtropical seas
DISTRIBUTION:	

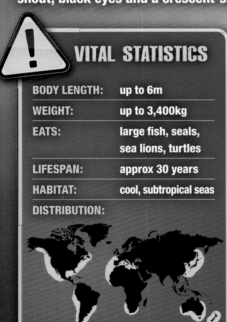

FIERCE PREDATOR

Great white sharks hunt a wide range of prey, including large fish, such as tuna, rays and smaller sharks, seals, sea lions, dolphins and sea turtles. Young sharks eat smaller fish and squid. The shark strikes at its prey from below, taking it by surprise, then catches it in its massive jaws. It then shakes its head from side to side, using its deadly teeth to saw chunks of flesh from its victim's body.

DID YOU KNOW?

Great white sharks have superb senses of smell for finding their prey. They can smell blood from hundreds of kilometres away, and can detect a single drop of blood in a million drops of water.

SPY HOPPING

Great white sharks sometimes lift their bodies and heads out of the water. This is called 'spy-hopping' and is also known among whales and dolphins. It allows the shark to look around for prey and other sharks.

SHARK ATTACKS

Great white sharks have a reputation for being ferocious man-eaters. But, in fact, they attack very few people each year. It is thought that these attacks happen when a shark mistakes a surfer or swimmer for its usual prey, such as seals and sea lions. A shark usually attacks at speed with a single bite, then backs away. Most attacks happen at dusk, when sharks are on the prowl for food.

Great whites are also known as WHITE POINTERS, BLUE POINTERS & WHITE DEATHS

DEADLY RATING

DID YOU KNOW?

Great white sharks are very rare because so many have been killed by humans or accidently caught in nets. The sharks are killed for their meat, jaws, and fins which are made into soup.

DEADLY FEATURES

Great white sharks have massive mouths, lined with triangular teeth with serrated cutting edges. The lower teeth keep the prey in place while the upper teeth tear off flesh. Like other sharks, great whites have several other rows of teeth, ready to replace any that break off.

EUNECTES MURINUS
GREEN ANACONDA

The green anaconda is the world's largest snake. It can grow to more than 9 metres in length and its stocky, muscular body is thicker than a human leg. Its skin is dark green, with a pattern of large, black spots. This provides the snake with excellent camouflage both in the water and on the rainforest floor.

⚠ VITAL STATISTICS

BODY LENGTH:	up to 9m
WEIGHT:	100–200 kg
EATS:	fish, birds, tapir, caimans, deer
LIFESPAN:	up to 10 years
HABITAT:	rainforest rivers
DISTRIBUTION:	

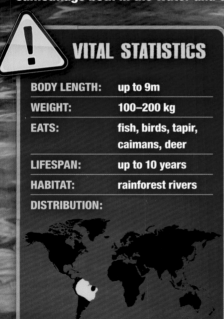

SWIMMING SKILLS

Anacondas spend most of their time in the water where they hunt for prey. They live mostly in shallow, slow-moving rainforest rivers and swamps in South America. They are superbly adapted for life in the water. Their eyes and nostrils are on top of their heads so that they can still see and breathe even when they are swimming or lying half-submerged in the water. Young anacondas are born in the water, and can swim straight away.

DID YOU KNOW?

Anacondas' upper and lower jaws are connected by ligaments that are very stretchy like elastic. This allows them to open their mouths wide enough to swallow prey many times as wide as their heads.

SNAKE PRINTS

The pattern of scales on the underside of an anaconda's tail is different in each snake. It can be used to identify individual snakes, just as fingerprints can in humans.

STEALTHY HUNTER

An anaconda hunts for its prey at night. It mainly eats fish, frogs, birds and sometimes larger animals such as deer, caimans and capybaras. It lies in the water, with just its snout showing. When prey comes near or stop at the water's edge to drink, the anaconda swims quickly towards it. It grabs it in its jaws, wraps its coils around it, then squeezes until its victim suffocates. Then it swallows it whole, head first. Anacondas occasionally hunt on land, although they move much more sluggishly. Smaller, younger anacondas have been found resting in trees, but fully grown female anacondas are much too heavy to climb trees.

Local names for anacondas are BULL KILLERS and ELEPHANT KILLERS because of their huge size.

DEADLY RATING

DEADLY FEATURES

Anacondas are not venomous. They belong to a group of snakes, called boas, that kill their prey by constriction (squeezing). Wrapped in an anaconda's massive coils, prey does not stand a chance and eventually stops breathing.

DID YOU KNOW?

It takes an anaconda a long time to digest its food. After a big meal, it may not need to eat again for weeks or even months.

CANIS LUPUS
GREY WOLF

Grey wolves are the largest wolves and live in packs of 4–7 animals, but packs may be as large as 20 animals. They are found mainly in North America and Asia, although once they were much more widespread. Members of the pack communicate by howling, an eerie sound that pierces the quiet of the forest at night.

VITAL STATISTICS

BODY LENGTH:	up to 1.6m
WEIGHT:	up to 80kg
EATS:	bison, elk, moose
LIFESPAN:	8–13 years
HABITAT:	grasslands, forests, tundra

DISTRIBUTION:

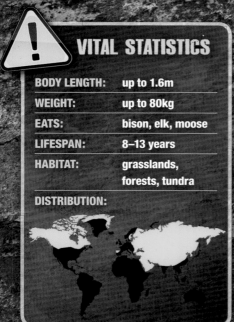

HUNTING IN PACKS

Wolves mostly hunt animals such as deer, moose and bison but also kill smaller animals. The pack hunts together, spreading out to surround its prey, then biting at its legs and rump. These bites make the animal bleed and slow it down so the wolves can bring it down. Although wolves will occasionally kill livestock, they rarely, if ever, attack people.

DID YOU KNOW?

Not all grey wolves have grey fur. In the Arctic, wolves have white fur that acts as camouflage, while in other places their fur can be reddish-brown or even black.

DEADLY FEATURES

The wolf's deadliest skill is its ability to work together in a pack. This allows it to run down and kill animals that would be too big for a single wolf to kill. It has strong senses of hearing and smell to help it to find prey.

DEADLY RATING

URSUS ARCTOS HORRIBILIS
GRIZZLY BEAR

Brown bears live in many parts of the world. The grizzly bear is a brown bear found in North American forests and coastal areas. It has thick fur and a hump of muscle over its shoulders that gives it the power to dig for food. It can rear up on its hind legs so it stands up to 2.5 metres tall.

! VITAL STATISTICS

BODY LENGTH:	up to 2.8m
WEIGHT:	80–600kg
EATS:	berries, squirrels, moose, salmon
LIFESPAN:	20–25 years
HABITAT:	tundra, forests
DISTRIBUTION:	

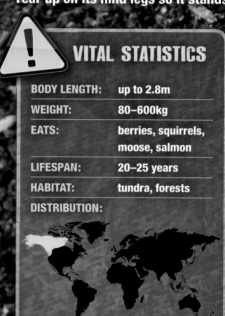

BEAR HUNT

The grizzly bear has a strong sense of smell that helps it to find food. Their sense of smell is a hundred times better than humans. These bears spend much of the time eating berries and other vegetation. But they can also eat meat and use their long claws to dig squirrels, marmots and other animals out of the ground. Other grizzly bears want a bigger meal and hunt for larger prey, such as moose (elk), wild sheep and goats.

SLEEPING BEARS

DID YOU KNOW?

Grizzly bears make dens where they spend the winter. Female bears give birth to their cubs during this time and often have twins.

In winter, grizzly bears enter their dens and go into a deep sleep. Their body temperature drops and they live off their fat stores. But it is not true hibernation because they can still move around. They wake up the following spring and must immediately start feeding to put on weight.

Grizzly bears get their name from the grizzled or grey hairs in their fur

FISHING BEARS

Many grizzly bears live along the coast of North America. When salmon swim up rivers and streams during the summer, these bears gather along the river banks. They use their claws to pull fish out of the water. Sometimes, the bears catch the salmon straight in their jaws as the fish leap up the river. They can eat many fish during this time to build up their fat reserves for the winter.

DID YOU KNOW?

Grizzly bears can run at around 48 kilometres per hour. They are also excellent climbers so anyone being chased is advised not to try climbing a tree to escape.

DEADLY FEATURES

A female grizzly is at her most deadly when she is defending her cubs. Her huge size and strength are terrifying and one blow from her paws can kill a large animal or human. The bear's long, curved claws are lethal weapons.

DEADLY RATING

PITOHUI DICHROUS
HOODED PITOHUI

There are at least three poisonous species of pitohui (pronounced 'pittoeey'), which are small, brightly coloured birds that live on the island of New Guinea. The hooded pitohui has a bright red/orange front and jet black head. The variable and rusty pitohui are also brightly coloured. But the birds' colours are not just for show – they may sound a warning.

VITAL STATISTICS

BODY LENGTH:	23cm
WEIGHT:	unknown
EATS:	insects, spiders
LIFESPAN:	unknown
HABITAT:	forests, woodlands

DISTRIBUTION:

PITOHUI POISON

The pitohui is the only poisonous bird in the world. Of the three known poisonous species, the hooded pitohui is the most toxic, and they all have poisonous skin and feathers. It is thought that the poison protects the birds from parasites, such as lice, and from predators, such as snakes and birds of prey.

DID YOU KNOW?

In Papua New Guinea, pitohuis are nicknamed 'rubbish birds' because their poison means that they are not good to eat.

DEADLY FEATURES

The pitohui's poison is similar to that found in the skin of the poison dart frog. The pitohuis do not make the poison themselves but most likely get it from the beetles they eat. In humans, the poison can cause numbness of the skin.

DEADLY RATING

☠ ☠ ☠ ☠ ☠

HIPPOPOTAMUS AMPHIBIUS
HIPPOPOTAMUS

The hippopotamus lives in and around the rivers and lakes of Africa. This huge plant-eating animal may look like a lumbering giant but it is one of the most dangerous animals in Africa, claiming far more lives than lions.

VITAL STATISTICS

BODY LENGTH:	3–5m
WEIGHT:	1800–3200kg
EATS:	grasses, sometimes eats dead animals
LIFESPAN:	30–40 years
HABITAT:	rivers and lakes
DISTRIBUTION:	

GRUMPY GIANT

The hippopotamus spends most of the day sleeping. It keeps out of the hot sun, wallowing in water or mud, and looks for food in the evening and at night. A hippo opens its huge mouth to show its large teeth when it feels threatened. It will charge at any animal that threatens its young or gets between the hippo and the water.

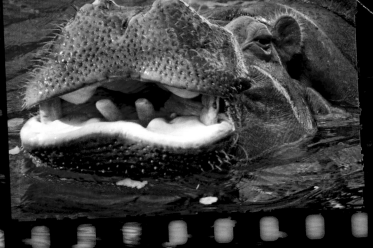

DEADLY FEATURES

DID YOU KNOW?

Hippos sink to the bottom of a river-bed and run along the bottom. Hippos are also fast runners on land and can move at 40 kilometres per hour, easily able to outrun a human!

Hippos are extremely aggressive creatures and are not afraid of most other animals. Their lethal weapons are their massive bulk and huge teeth. A hippo's lower canines can measure 50 cm long and can crush a boat.

PANTHERA ONCA
JAGUAR

The jaguar is the biggest cat in South America. It usually lives in tropical rainforest, where it can climb trees to hide and hunt. Its spotted fur is perfect camouflage as it stalks its prey through the shadows. Jaguars can also have black fur and these are often wrongly called 'black panthers'.

⚠ VITAL STATISTICS

BODY LENGTH:	1.6–1.8m
WEIGHT:	36–140kg
EATS:	deer, tapir, turtles, snakes, fish
LIFESPAN:	up to 11 years
HABITAT:	tropical rainforests
DISTRIBUTION:	

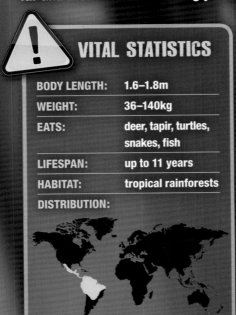

JAGUAR JAWS

The jaguar has a powerful, muscular body and extremely strong jaws. It lies in wait for prey and jumps out when a victim comes near. The jaguar is a good swimmer and will wait at a river's edge to spring at turtles, fish and caimans in the water. It can swim carrying a large kill and often drags prey up a tree to eat later.

DID YOU KNOW?

The word jaguar comes form the American Indian word 'yaguara' which means 'killer that takes its prey in a single bound'.

DEADLY FEATURES

The jaguar's stealth makes it a deadly predator. Its teeth are so strong that it can crack open a turtle's shell. It kills many animals by biting right through their skulls.

DEADLY RATING

APIS MELLIFERA SCUTELLATA LEPELETIER
KILLER BEE

'Killer' bee is the name given to the Africanized bee. It came about when bee-keepers in Brazil tried to breed African bees to produce extra honey. Some of the African bees were accidently released into the wild. They bred with local European bees and created a new type of 'killer' bee.

VITAL STATISTICS

BODY LENGTH:	nearly 2cm
WEIGHT:	0.1g
EATS:	nectar and pollen
LIFESPAN:	queen bees can live up to 2 years
HABITAT:	nests in many places
DISTRIBUTION:	

KILLER SWARMS

'Killer' bees are found in South, Central and the southern part of North America. They are deadly because they defend their nests fiercely against anything they see as a threat, forming swarms and stinging. People disturbing their nests, or loud noises, can trigger this defensive reaction.

DEADLY RATING

DID YOU KNOW?

'Killer' bees are slightly smaller than European honey bees. Soldier bees respond to any disturbance and alert the colony to defend its nest.

DEADLY FEATURES

The 'killer' bee's sting is no stronger than an ordinary honey bee sting which can be painful but not dangerous. However, because killer bees attack in a swarm, they are extremely dangerous. They will also follow a victim over a long distance.

ORCINUS ORCA
KILLER WHALE

Killer whales, or orcas, are found in all of the world's oceans, from the Arctic Ocean in the far north to the Southern Ocean in the far south. Famous for their striking black-and-white markings, they live in groups, called pods, of up to 40 animals. The members of a pod stay together for life.

⚠ VITAL STATISTICS

BODY LENGTH:	4–9m
WEIGHT:	3–5 tonnes
EATS:	fish, seals, squid, whale calves
LIFESPAN:	30–70 years
HABITAT:	Oceans worldwide
DISTRIBUTION:	

WHALE HUNT

Like wolves, killer whales hunt together in packs. This allows them to catch large animals, such as other whales. The killer whales chase a calf and its mother until their victims are exhausted. Then they separate the calf and stop it reaching the surface to breathe. Killer whales are opportunistic hunters, but in some areas they may become specialised and mainly hunt one type of prey depending on the habitat.

DID YOU KNOW?

Killer whales sometimes throw their prey of seals into the air or slap them with their tails to stun and kill them before eating them.

DEADLY FEATURES

Apart from their size and strength, killer whales are also among the fastest animals in the sea. When chasing prey, they can swim at speeds of 56km/h. They have conical, interlocking teeth for catching prey.

DEADLY RATING

OPHIOPHAGUS HANNAH
KING COBRA

The world's longest venomous snake, the king cobra lives in India and parts of South Eastern Asia. It is found near streams in rainforests and mangrove swamps where it spends the day hunting for its prey of other snakes and lizards. It locates its prey by smell and sight, then chases after it and strikes.

VITAL STATISTICS

BODY LENGTH:	3.5–5.5m
WEIGHT:	6kg
EATS:	other snakes, lizards
LIFESPAN:	20 years
HABITAT:	rainforests, mangrove swamps

DISTRIBUTION:

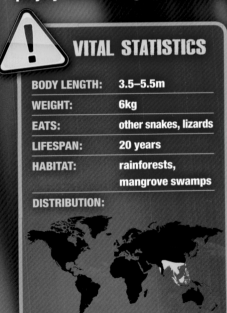

SNAKE SKIN

A king cobra is a powerfully-built snake, reaching 5.5 metres in length. It is the longest venomous snake. Adults have greenish-brown and black skin, with yellow or white markings and a cream or pale yellow belly. Young cobras are black with yellow bands. Even though it is a large snake, a king cobra is remarkably fast-moving and agile.

UNDER THREAT?

Although not officially classified as endangered, king cobras are under threat from destruction of their habitat by deforestation. They are also persecuted by people who are afraid of them and who also use their skin, meat and bile for traditional medicine.

DID YOU KNOW?

When threatened, a king cobra lifts its body off the ground to a height of about 1.5 metres. Then it spreads out its hood like a fan and growls.

The king cobra's Latin/scientific name means 'SNAKE-EATER' after its favourite prey

EGGS AND YOUNG

A female cobra is particularly deadly when she is guarding her nest. King cobras are caring parents, making complex nests from piles of leaves, grass and soil. The female then makes a hole in the top, lays 20–40 eggs and covers them with leaves. She sits on top and guards the nest fiercely until the eggs hatch. The male also stays nearby. Baby cobras can already bite as soon as they hatch.

DID YOU KNOW?

Unlike most snakes, the king cobra does not make a hissing sound when it is threatened. Instead, it makes a deep growling noise from its throat.

DEADLY FEATURES

A king cobra has two short, fixed fangs at the front of its mouth. These inject venom, made in its salivary glands, into its prey. It can produce enough poison in a single bite to kill 20–30 adult humans or an adult Asian elephant.

DEADLY RATING

VARANUS KOMODOENSIS
KOMODO DRAGON

The mighty Komodo dragon is the largest lizard in the world. Growing up to 3 metres long, it has a heavy, stocky body with short, strong legs and a long, muscular tail. It is very rare and is found only on the island of Komodo and a few other islands in Indonesia.

! VITAL STATISTICS

BODY LENGTH:	up to 3m
WEIGHT:	50–160kg
EATS:	carrion, deer, wild pigs, birds
LIFESPAN:	30–50 years
HABITAT:	grasslands
DISTRIBUTION:	

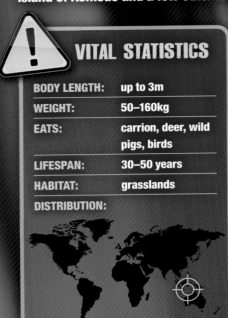

DRAGON DIET

Komodo dragons mainly eat carrion (the bodies of dead animals). But they are also ferocious hunters, ambushing large animals, such as deer, goats and wild pigs. They grab their prey in their sharp claws, then give a lethal bite to the underside or throat. Then they follow the injured animal until it dies, and tear it apart with their sharp, serrated teeth.

DEADLY RATING

DID YOU KNOW?

Young Komodo dragons spend their first few months living high up in the trees to avoid falling prey to predators, including cannibalistic adults.

DEADLY FEATURES

A Komodo dragon's saliva contains more than 50 different kinds of lethal bacteria. These are injected into prey as the dragon bites and cause deadly infections and, eventually, death.

PANTHERA PARDUS
LEOPARD

The leopard lives in Africa and some parts of Asia. Its spotted fur makes it very hard to see, as can the fact that it often hides high up in the branches of a tree. It uses its stealth and camouflage to hunt its prey at night.

 VITAL STATISTICS

BODY LENGTH:	up to 2.9m
WEIGHT:	37–90kg
EATS:	antelope, wildebeest
LIFESPAN:	10–15 years
HABITAT:	forests, mountains, grasslands

DISTRIBUTION:

LONELY LEOPARDS

The leopard usually lives and hunts alone. It is an expert at stalking and hiding from prey, and is superbly camouflaged. The leopard hunts many different animals, including gazelles, wildebeest and jackals. It leaps on its prey and bites its throat so that it suffocates. Leopards are extremely strong and will drag large prey, sometimes 2–3 times their own bodyweight, up into a tree to stop other animals eating it.

DEADLY FEATURES

The leopard's camouflage makes it very hard to spot. This means that it can creep up on prey without any warning. It also has a massive skull, powerful jaw muscles and, like all big cats, large, sharp canine teeth.

DEADLY RATING

PANTHERA LEO
LION

The African lion is the only big cat to live in a group, called a pride. In each pride there may be around three male lions and a larger number of lionesses and their cubs. The lionesses in a pride work together to look after their cubs. The lionesses also hunt as a group, and stalk and kill prey for the pride.

VITAL STATISTICS

BODY LENGTH:	1.6–2.5m
WEIGHT:	126–272kg
EATS:	zebra, antelope, wildebeest, buffalo
LIFESPAN:	12–18 years
HABITAT:	grasslands, forests
DISTRIBUTION:	

MIGHTY MALES

The male lions in a pride rarely get involved in hunting but they are still deadly. Part of their job is to keep the pride's territory safe from other lions. They do this by marking the area with scent and roaring loudly. Male lions are the only big cats to have manes, which help to make them look bigger and fiercer. They fight each other to decide who is in charge of the pride.

LEARNER LIONS

DID YOU KNOW?

When a new male lion joins a pride, he sometimes kills all the cubs. This is to make sure that any new lions in the pride are his own cubs.

Lion cubs learn to hunt by play-fighting with each other, pouncing at twigs and trying to catch the end of their mother's tail. They start going out on hunts with their mother when they are about three months old. By the age of two, they can hunt for themselves.

TEAM WORK

Lionesses have to hunt together as a team because
most of their prey is bigger or can run faster than them.
They creep up on a herd of prey animals, such as zebra
or wildebeest, crouching silently behind the grass and
scrub. Then they slowly move in closer. When they have
singled out a victim and surrounded it, one lioness runs
in for the kill. Then the others join her to prevent the
animal escaping and to finish the job.

DID YOU KNOW?

Once the pride has made a kill, the male lions get to eat first. The lionesses eat what is left, followed by the cubs.

DEADLY FEATURES

Lions often eat prey that is much bigger than them. To catch and kill large animals, a lion has powerful muscles for running over short distances, strong jaws, sharp teeth and uses incredible strength to pull down its victim.

DEADLY RATING

CULICIDAE
MOSQUITO

There are over 3,000 types of mosquito found worldwide. Despite their size, some types are deadly to humans, causing more deaths in Africa than any other creature. Most of these deaths are caused by malaria, a disease spread when an Anopheles mosquito bites.

VITAL STATISTICS

BODY LENGTH:	3–20mm
WEIGHT:	2.5mg
EATS:	blood, nectar
LIFESPAN:	up to 6 months
HABITAT:	freshwater in warm climates

DISTRIBUTION:

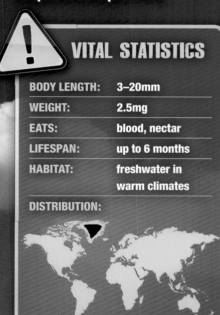

BLOODSUCKERS

Mosquitoes breed in shallow water. Although notorious for feeding on blood, their main source of food is nectar. Only females feed on blood, which is an important source of protein and iron for their eggs. They feed mainly at dawn and dusk. As the mosquito bites, it pricks two tubes into the victim's skin. One sucks up blood and the other produces saliva to stop the blood clotting so that it will flow until the mosquito is full. It is the saliva that transmits diseases to humans.

DEADLY RATING

DID YOU KNOW?

Malaria is not the only disease spread by mosquitoes. Different species can spread a variety of diseases such as encephalitis, elephantiasis, yellow fever and the West Nile virus.

DEADLY FEATURES

The mosquito's special senses help it to find its victims by locating movement, breathing and sweat. The different types of mosquito have unintentionally caused the deaths of millions of humans worldwide.

DENDROBATIDAE
POISON DART FROG

Poison dart frogs are a group of frogs that live in the tropical rainforests of Central and South America. Most species are tiny but deadly, thanks to the poison they carry in their brightly-coloured skins. There are around 200 different species of poison dart frogs.

VITAL STATISTICS

BODY LENGTH:	1.5–4cm
WEIGHT:	2–7g
EATS:	ants, beetles, other insects
LIFESPAN:	7–10 years
HABITAT:	rainforests
DISTRIBUTION:	

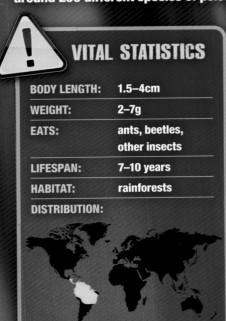

WARNING COLOURS

Poison dart frogs come in a range of bright colours, including red, green, blue, black and golden. Their colours make them easy to spot as they search for their insect prey during the day. But their striking colours are not simply for decoration. They are a warning to possible predators that the frogs are highly poisonous and should be left well alone.

DID YOU KNOW?

Poison dart frogs get their name because poison from their skin is used by local rainforest people to tip their blow darts for hunting monkeys, jaguars and birds.

WATER BABIES

Poison dart frogs lay their eggs in damp places on leaves, plants and roots. When the tadpoles hatch, some parents carry them on their backs to water where they can grow into frogs.

GOLDEN FROG (*Phyllobates terribilis*)

The golden poison dart frog lives in a tiny patch of rainforest in Colombia. It is one of the largest and deadliest of the poison dart frogs. In fact, it is thought to be one of the most poisonous land animals. Adults have a bright, golden colour with dark spots. They live on the rainforest floor, often close to streams but also have sticky pads on their feet for climbing trees. They feed on insects which they catch with their long, sticky tongues.

DEADLY RATING

DEADLY FEATURES

DID YOU KNOW?

The golden poison dart frog is deadly to most animals. But one rainforest snake is resistant to the frog's poison and can eat it, although it is not totally safe from being harmed.

The golden poison dart frog stores its poison in special glands scattered across its skin. A single frog contains enough poison to kill up to 20 adult humans or 10,000 mice. Its poison works quickly, attacking the nerves and muscles, and causing heart failure.

URSUS MARITIMUS
POLAR BEAR

The polar bear is the largest bear, and usually lives alone on the ice in the Arctic polar region. It has thick white fur that is water-repellent and acts as camouflage on the ice. Compared to other bears, the polar bear's neck is very long and it has huge paddle-like feet.

VITAL STATISTICS

BODY LENGTH:	1.9–2.6m
WEIGHT:	150–800kg
EATS:	seals, walruses, birds
LIFESPAN:	25–30 years
HABITAT:	Arctic pack ice
DISTRIBUTION:	

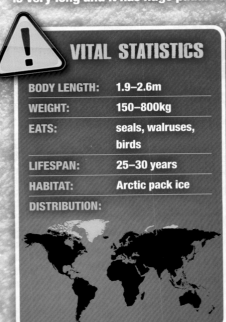

SEAL HUNTER

The polar bear's main prey is the ringed seal. These seals swim under the ice looking for fish, but they have to come up to holes in the ice when they need air. The polar bear waits patiently by a breathing hole or a crack in the ice. When it sees a seal come up for air, it pounces. Sometimes, the bear swims under the ice to catch seals or it stalks and attacks them as they rest on the surface of the ice.

DID YOU KNOW?

A polar bear's skin is black under its white fur. This dark skin helps the bear to absorb as much heat as possible in such a cold climate. A thick layer of blubber (fat) also helps to keep it warm.

UNDER THREAT

Polar bears are in serious danger of becoming extinct. This is because global warming is melting the Arctic ice. The bears depend on the ice for hunting. Without it, they risk starvation unless they can adapt to life on land.

SCAVENGER

Another way in which the polar bear finds food is by scavenging. It often eats the carcasses of dead walruses and whales that have been washed up on the ice, or the remains of other bears' kills. When polar bears find themselves living near humans, they sometimes raid rubbish bins to find food. It can be very dangerous for people to come across a hungry bear.

In the Inuit language, the polar bear is called NANOOK. In Inuit mythology, Nanook was the master of the bears

DEADLY RATING

DEADLY FEATURES

DID YOU KNOW?

The soles of a polar bear's feet are covered in fur and small bumps called papillae. This helps to keep its feet warm on the ice and stops them slipping.

The polar bear is an amazing hunter. Its powerful sense of smell helps it to find prey, while its white fur provides camouflage as it hunts. It can run and swim incredible distances and has strength, sharp claws and deadly teeth to destroy its victims.

PHYSALIA PHYSALIS
PORTUGUESE MAN-O'-WAR

The Portuguese man-o'-war looks like a jellyfish. In fact, it is a siphonophore, made up of four different kinds of animal, called polyps. The man-o'-war lives in warm water in the Atlantic, Pacific and Indian Oceans. It cannot swim but its sail-like body is blown by the wind or drifts on the ocean currents.

VITAL STATISTICS

BODY LENGTH:	up to 30cm; tentacles 10–50m
WEIGHT:	unknown
EATS:	young fish, shrimps
LIFESPAN:	unknown
HABITAT:	warm seas
DISTRIBUTION:	

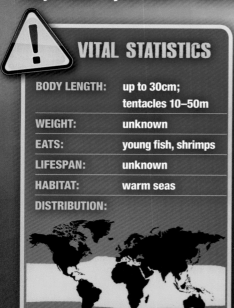

SEAFOOD DIET

The Portuguese man-o'-war preys mainly on small fish, young fish, shrimps and crustaceans which it traps in its stinging tentacles (see below). The tentacles trail from the man-o'-war's body and can measure up to 50 metres long. They 'fish' through the water, hoping to catch prey. Then they contract (get shorter) to pull the prey towards the mouth.

DID YOU KNOW?

A tiny fish (*Nomeus gronovii*) lives among the man-o'-war's tentacles and even picks food off them. It is not harmed by the man-o'-war's venom.

DEADLY FEATURES

The man-o'-war's tentacles are covered in venom-filled cells which are used to sting and kill prey, and in self defence. Tentacles can still sting for hours or even days after a man-o'-war is dead.

DEADLY RATING

TETRAODONTIDAE
PUFFER FISH

With over 120 different species, puffer fish are found all over the world in warm oceans. Most are small- to medium-sized but some can measure up to 90 centimetres. Although not all puffer fish are poisonous, many are very dangerous and these are thought to be the second most poisonous vertebrates after poison dart frogs.

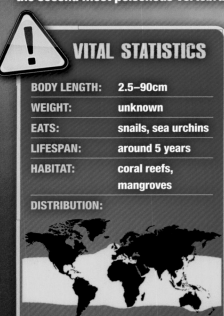

VITAL STATISTICS

BODY LENGTH:	2.5–90cm
WEIGHT:	unknown
EATS:	snails, sea urchins
LIFESPAN:	around 5 years
HABITAT:	coral reefs, mangroves

DISTRIBUTION:

BALLOON FISH

Unlike the porcupine fish, which has long conspicuous spines that stick out when attacked, a puffer fish's body is covered in tiny spines that are almost like sandpaper. If it is attacked by a predator, it gulps in mouthfuls of water or air and blows itself up like a balloon so that it looks much bigger than it is. Very few animals will try to eat it or even be able to get their mouths round it.

DEADLY RATING

☠ ☠ ☠ ☠

DEADLY FEATURES

Few puffer fish have poisonous spines; it is the skin, liver and intestines of puffer fish that contain a deadly toxin called tetrodoxin, which is believed to be 1000 times more powerful than cyanide. If eaten, they can cause paralysis and stop a person from breathing.

DID YOU KNOW?

Puffer fish can blow themselves up to 2–3 times their normal size. In order to do this, they have very stretchy skin.

PYGOCENTRUS NATTERERI
RED-BELLIED PIRANHA

Piranhas have razor-sharp teeth and a reputation for being ferocious. In the movies, they are shown hunting in shoals, stripping the flesh from their victims' bones in a feeding frenzy. It seems, though, that swimming in shoals is not a form of defence but helps to keep them safe from predators.

VITAL STATISTICS

BODY LENGTH:	up to 33cm
WEIGHT:	up to 3.5kg
EATS:	fish, insects, crustaceans
LIFESPAN:	8–12 years
HABITAT:	rivers, streams
DISTRIBUTION:	

PIRANHA SHOAL

Red-bellied piranhas live in rainforest rivers and streams in South America. They have reddish-brown sides and bellies, and silver-grey backs. During the day, they gather in shoals of 20–30 to wait for prey. They mostly hunt fish, snails and insects. They also scavenge on dead and injured animals. They find their prey by smell or movement, using a set of sensors down the sides of their bodies.

DID YOU KNOW?

Some types of piranhas are vegetarians. They eat seeds and fruit that fall into the river from the bankside trees. Others specialise in eating the fins and scales of other fish.

DEADLY FEATURES

A piranha's sharp, pointed teeth are deadly weapons, used for killing and eating prey. The teeth are tightly packed and lock together. If one tooth breaks off, another grows in its place. Rainforest people use piranha teeth for making tools.

CROCODYLUS POROSUS
SALTWATER CROCODILE

The saltwater crocodile is enormous. Growing up to 7 metres in length, it is the largest crocodile and also the largest reptile in the world. It lives in rivers and along coasts in South East Asia, Australia and around the Pacific Ocean. This giant is superbly adapted for hunting its prey in the water, with a long, powerful tail, webbed back feet and crushing jaws.

VITAL STATISTICS

BODY LENGTH:	3–7m
WEIGHT:	400–1000kg
EATS:	birds, mammals, reptiles, fish, crabs
LIFESPAN:	over 60 years
HABITAT:	rivers, coasts
DISTRIBUTION:	

KILLER CROC

A saltwater crocodile is a carnivore, feeding on birds, mammals and reptiles. It lies almost completely submerged in the water, hiding from its prey. Its eyes, ears and nostrils are on top of its head so that it can still see, hear and breathe. It can also block off its throat so that it can open its mouth underwater without drowning. When its prey gets near, it lunges out of water, grabs it and drags it underwater to eat.

DID YOU KNOW?

Saltwater crocodiles have been hunted for their meat, eggs and skin, and also threatened by the loss of their habitats. In Australia, some are taken from the wild and moved to farms for breeding.

CROC COMS

To communicate with each other, saltwater crocodiles use a series of barking calls. Hatchlings give a short, high bark. Adults hiss or cough if they feel threatened, and give a long, low growl to attract mates.

NESTS AND BABIES

A female saltwater crocodile lays her 40–60 eggs in a mound-like nest made from mud and plants and built close to the water. She guards the nest fiercely for three months until the eggs hatch. As soon as she hears the newly-hatched crocodiles chirping, she digs them out of the nest and carries them to water in her mouth so that they can learn to swim.

A group of saltwater crocodiles is known as a BASK (on land) and a FLOAT (in the water)

DEADLY RATING

☠ ☠ ☠ ☠ ☠

DEADLY FEATURES

DID YOU KNOW?

Saltwater crocodiles are strong swimmers. They sometimes travel long distances out to sea, and have been found over 1,000 kilometres from land.

A saltwater crocodile's sheer size makes it a deadly predator. It is strong enough to drag a fully-grown water buffalo into the water. Its powerful jaws can snap shut with massive force, and are lined with 60 or more sharp teeth.

DASYATIS BREVICAUDATA
SHORT-TAIL STINGRAY

Stingrays are fish, related to sharks. They are found in warm, tropical seas, usually close to the shore. Some also live in rivers. The short-tailed stingray lives in the Indian and Pacific Oceans. It has a large, flat, diamond-shaped body, measuring up to 2 metres across its 'wings', and 4 metres in length, including its tail.

VITAL STATISTICS

BODY LENGTH:	4m (including tail)
WEIGHT:	350kg
EATS:	crabs, shrimps, eels, molluscs
LIFESPAN:	unknown
HABITAT:	coastal waters
DISTRIBUTION:	

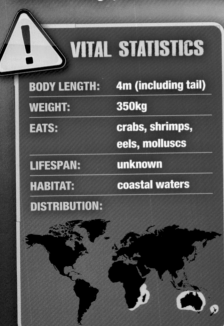

STING IN THE TAIL

The stingray's tail has a long, sharp spike, used in self defence. Underneath the spike are grooves that make venom. If the stingray is attacked or disturbed, it can suddenly whip its tail around and stick its spike into its victim. Stingrays are usually placid, however, and will only attack if they feel under threat.

DID YOU KNOW?

Stingrays find their food of molluscs, crustaceans and small fish by smell and using electrical patterns in the water. Then they stir up the sandy sea bed with their wings to uncover their prey.

DEADLY FEATURES

A stingray's spike is needle-sharp and armed with tiny barbs. It can grow more than 40 centimetres long. It can cause serious injuries in humans, and sometimes kill, if it pierces a vital organ, such as the heart.

DEADLY RATING

SYNANCEIA VERRUCOSA
STONEFISH

The most venomous fish in the world, the stonefish lives in shallow water along the coasts of the Indian and Pacific Oceans. Its body is mottled brown and grey, with flaps of skin and wart-like bumps. Lying on the sea bed, it blends in with its background and looks exactly like a weed-covered rock.

VITAL STATISTICS

BODY LENGTH:	up to 35cm
WEIGHT:	1.5kg
EATS:	fish, shrimps
LIFESPAN:	5–10 years
HABITAT:	along coasts, coral reefs

DISTRIBUTION:

STONEFISH SELF DEFENCE

Stonefish are preyed on by sharks and rays, and have a lethal form of self defence. Sticking up from their back is a row of 13 sharp spines. If anything touches the spines, they lock upright and shoot deadly venom into the attacker.

DEADLY FEATURES

DID YOU KNOW?

Wearing thick-soled shoes can help to protect against a stonefish attack. But it still pays to tread very carefully – the spines are strong enough to pierce tough rubber.

The stonefish's venomous spines and camouflage are a deadly combination. Swimmers can easily tread on a stonefish, mistaking it for a stone. In humans, the venom causes muscle weakness, shock and terrible pain. Stings are rarely fatal.

SARCOPHILUS HARRISII
TASMANIAN DEVIL

The Tasmanian devil is the size of a small dog and lives on the island of Tasmania, off Australia. Stockily built, with dark brown fur, it was given its alarming name because of its extremely loud and terrifying screeching. Despite a ferocious reputation, the Tasmanian devil is actually quite shy and will only aggressively defend itself if threatened.

⚠ VITAL STATISTICS

BODY LENGTH:	52–80 cm
WEIGHT:	12–18 kg
EATS:	dead animals, small mammals, insects
LIFESPAN:	5–6 years
HABITAT:	coastal heath, forests
DISTRIBUTION:	

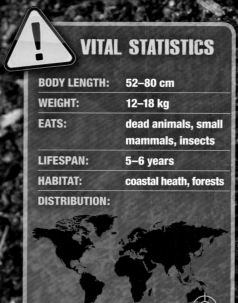

DEVIL ATTACK

Tasmanian devils emerge at night to look for food. They hunt small animals, such as possums and wombats but are also scavengers, locating dead animals with their superb sense of smell. When threatened, a Tasmanian Devil 'yawns' showing off its powerful teeth. Then it growls, screeches and attacks.

DID YOU KNOW?

Tasmanian devils are marsupials, like kangaroos, koalas and possums. They carry their young in a pouch until they are big enough to fend for themselves.

DEADLY FEATURES

Tasmanian devils have powerful jaws filled with sharp, strong teeth for biting through flesh and crushing bones. Their defensive aggression and fierce appearance helps scare away other animals.

ENDANGERED SPECIES

DEADLY RATING

GALEOCERDO CUVIER
TIGER SHARK

One of the largest sharks in the world, the tiger shark gets its name from the dark stripes running down the sides of its body. These are easier to see on younger sharks but tend to fade with age. Second only to the great white in its fearsome reputation, tiger sharks have large heads and rounded snouts, filled with deadly teeth.

VITAL STATISTICS

BODY LENGTH:	2–5.5m
WEIGHT:	385–635kg
EATS:	fish, seals, sea birds
LIFESPAN:	45–50 years
HABITAT:	coastal waters in warm seas

DISTRIBUTION:

SOLITARY HUNTER

Tiger sharks are found all over the world in tropical and warm waters. They usually hunt alone, at night. They swim inshore to hunt, returning to deeper waters during the day. Tiger sharks look sluggish but are fast swimmers and can reach speeds of more than 30 km/h, though only in short bursts. They have excellent eyesight but rely on their superb sense of smell to find prey.

DID YOU KNOW?

A female shark may give birth to litters of 10–80 pups. Each pup measures 50–75 centimetres long. The pups hatch from eggs inside their mother's body, then are born live.

SACRED SHARKS

Tiger sharks are sacred in Hawaii where they are believed to be the spirits of ancestors with magical powers. Despite this, thousands of sharks have been killed to make the sea safer for tourists and swimmers.

DUSTBIN DIET

Tiger sharks are famous for their huge appetites and their ability to eat almost anything. This has earned them the nickname of 'garbage sharks'. Their prey mainly includes fish, sea turtles, smaller sharks, all kinds of seabirds, seals and sea lions. They also actively hunt smaller sharks, including other tiger sharks. But more unusual objects, such as lumps of wood, bags of potatoes, car tyres and even a suit of armour have been found inside a tiger shark's stomach. Tiger sharks have also been known to attack people.

DID YOU KNOW?

Apart from stripes, young tiger sharks may also have dark blotches or spots, and are also known as leopard sharks or spotted sharks.

DEADLY FEATURES

Tiger sharks have large, flat and extremely sharp teeth with finely serrated edges. These teeth are strong enough to bite through bones and turtle shells. They are also curious and aggressive creatures, making them even more dangerous.

DEADLY RATING

DESMODUS ROTUNDUS
VAMPIRE BAT

Vampire bats live in Central and South America and, due to their portrayal in films, are one of the most misunderstood animals. They live in colonies that normally include up to 100 bats, although colonies of 5,000 have been reported. At night, they search for animals to prey on, such as cattle, horses and occasionally humans.

VITAL STATISTICS

BODY LENGTH:	up to 9cm
WEIGHT:	up to 50g
EATS:	blood of animals
LIFESPAN:	up to 12 years
HABITAT:	caves, tree hollows
DISTRIBUTION:	

CREEPY CRAWLY

A vampire bat can also hop and jump to reach prey that is much larger than itself. It is very important that the bat's victim does not wake, as the bat is so small that it would have trouble defending itself if attacked.

DID YOU KNOW?

Vampire bats almost never kill their victims, but they occasionally carry and spread deadly infections and diseases such as rabies when they bite other animals.

DAYTIME REST

During the day, a colony of vampire bats sleep in darkness, hanging upside down from their roosts in the roofs of caves. In the deep of night, they wake up and go out hunting.

BLOOD-DRINKER

When the vampire bat has found its victim and climbed on, it prepares to feed. It flattens any hairs in the way by licking the skin. Then it uses its sharp front teeth to make a small cut, only millimetres across, in the skin and uses its tongue to lap up the blood. The bat's saliva stops the blood from clotting so that it keeps flowing until the bat is full.

DID YOU KNOW?

When a vampire bat has had a big meal of blood, it can be too heavy to take off and fly away. It jumps to get itself off the ground and launch itself into flight.

DEADLY FEATURES

A vampire bats detects its prey through echolocation, smell and sound. When it has found a suitable host, it uses special heat sensors on its nose to detect the best place to feed. The bats teeth are so small that the victim does not feel a thing.

DEADLY RATING

PELAMIS PLATURUS
YELLOW-BELLY SEA SNAKE

The deadliest snakes in the world are found in the warm waters of the Indian and Pacific Oceans. They are superbly adapted to life in the sea. They use their flattened tails as paddles for swimming and can stay underwater for 30 minutes to two hours at a time, closing their nostrils to keep water out.

VITAL STATISTICS

BODY LENGTH:	1–1.5m
WEIGHT:	1.5kg
EATS:	fish, fish eggs, molluscs, crustaceans
LIFESPAN:	4–5 years
HABITAT:	tropical coastal waters
DISTRIBUTION:	

SHY SNAKES

Sea snakes forage for food during the day. Their main prey is fish, particularly eels, fish eggs, molluscs and crustaceans. On coral reefs, they use their small heads to pull eels from the sandy sea bed. Sea snakes use a poisonous bite to kill their prey. They also use their venom in self defence, although they are usually shy and only bite if provoked.

DEADLY RATING

☠ ✖ ☠ ✖ ☠ ✖ ☠

DEADLY FEATURES

DID YOU KNOW?

Sea snakes sometimes gather in huge groups, thousands strong. It is thought that they do this to breed. After storms, large numbers may be washed up on the beach.

Most sea snakes are deadly poisonous. The yellow-bellied sea snake's venom is 10 times stronger than a cobra's. But the snakes have tiny fangs and only inject small amounts of venom in each bite.

LOOK OUT FOR THESE FANTASTIC

CHILDREN'S BOOKS

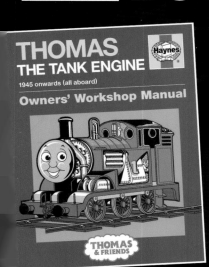

THOMAS THE TANK ENGINE
1945 onwards (all aboard)
Owners' Workshop Manual
THOMAS & FRIENDS

ROARY THE RACING CAR
Silverhatch Raceway's Number 1 Star!
Owners' Workshop Manual

BATTLE of BRITAIN
STICKER and ACTIVITY BOOK

PIRATE Manual
LOADS FOR YOUNG PIRATES TO MAKE AND DO
Andrew Parkinson

SPY Manual
LOADS FOR YOUNG SPIES TO MAKE AND DO
Andrew Parkinson
TOP SECRET

POCKET MANUAL
The history of the British monarchy
KINGS & QUEENS

POCKET MANUAL
The world's most dangerous predators
DEADLY CREATURES

POCKET MANUAL
Teams and players, facts and figures
WORLD CUP FOOTBALL

POCKET MANUAL
The fastest road and racing cars on Earth
WORLD'S FASTEST CARS

www.haynes.co.uk

Anita Ganeri and Charlotte Guillain have asserted their right to
be identified as the authors of this book.

Published in August 2010.

British Library Cataloguing-in-Publication Data:
A catalogue record for this book is available from
the British Library

ISBN 978 1 84425 968 7

Published by Haynes Publishing,
Sparkford, Yeovil, Somerset BA22 7JJ, UK
Tel: 01963 442030 Fax: 01963 440001
Int. tel: +44 1963 442030 Int. fax: +44 1963 440001
Email: sales@haynes.co.uk
Website: www.haynes.co.uk

Haynes North America, Inc.,
861 Lawrence Drive, Newbury Park
California 91320, USA

Design: Richard Parsons

Alamy: 11, 29, 33, 49, 61, 81, 103, 124, 125
Claire Waring: 75
D&R Halfacre: 7, 89
istockphoto.com: 15, 16, 21, 23, 24, 41, 43, 45, 55, 65,
67, 69, 77, 79, 83, 85, 101, 111, 119, 127
Oceanwide images 30, 37-39, 51, 53, 57, 59, 113
All other images from Wikimedia Commons

Printed and bound in the USA

The Author

Anita Ganeri is an award-winning author of children's information
books, covering a wide range of subjects. In 2009, she won the
Blue Peter Book Award for the Best Book with Facts. She lives in
the north of England with her family and dogs.

POCKET MANUAL

The world's most dangerous animals

DEADLY CREATURES

D1420273